Gallery Books
Editor: Peter Fallon

THE STONE JUG

Frank McGuinness

THE STONE JUG

Gallery Books

The Stone Jug
is first published
simultaneously in paperback
and in a clothbound edition
on 4 December 2003.

The Gallery Press
Loughcrew
Oldcastle
County Meath
Ireland

ISBN 1 85235 352 X (*paperback*)
    1 85235 353 8 (*clothbound*)

A CIP catalogue record for this book
is available from the British Library.

The Gallery Press acknowledges the financial assistance
of An Chomhairle Ealaíon / The Arts Council, Ireland.

Contents

PART ONE
Fahan Hill
  Fahan Hill *page* 13
  Sorn 16
  The Stone Jug 17
  Cockhill 18
  Fisherman 19
  Ardraven 20
  Perry Como 21
  Umracam 22
  Ivy 23

PART TWO
Gyrfalcon
  Hello 27
  Goodbye 28
  Leaves 29
  Rich 30
  Poor 31
  Butter and Tar 32
  The Jewish Bride 33
  Survivor 34
  Angelus 35
  Wings 36
  Nine Times Nine 37
  Mind 38
  Car 39
  Law 40
  Malin Head 41
  Horse's Head 42
  Father Hegarty's Rock 43
  The Rhythm Boys 44
  March 45
  Oranges 46
  With 47

Purgatory 48
Lie 49
Truth 50
Sasparilla 51
Shamrock 52
Clay 53
Roar 54
Dream 55
Dreaming 56
The Bali Sea 57
St Roche 58
Laughter 59
Glove 60
Nightmares 61
Ibsen in Winter 62
Drum 63
Prog 64
Pain 65
You 66
Ghost 67
Damned 68
Father 69
Lover 70
Fate 71
Possessed 72
Run 73
Orchids 74
Herbs 75
Leg 76
East 77
West 78
Paint 79
Fists 80
Judge 81
Apples 82

Aisling 83
End 84
Clean 85
Soon 86

PART THREE
The Wife's Lament
The Wife's Lament 89
The Husband's Message 91
Cure 93
Riddle 94
Elegy 95
Gardens in Winter: A Charm 96

for Kaye and John Fanning

PART ONE

Fahan Hill

Fahan Hill

Master McAteer taught us Geography.
The Irish for Dundalk, *Dún Dealgan*.
The fort of what — I forget. Crown of thorn,
those red days. I stopped learning. Too late to cry.
He did his best, time of forgiveness.
I wish I believed in forgiveness. No.
Sorrow is the way of the saints. Sinner,
I will spit on the rod. North, south, east, west,
my hard town, my home town, thirty years ago,
spalpeen, I left you, my scythe, my dinner.

I ate iron to make me what I am.
I digested clay. My breakfast of dock-
leaves left me hungry for the scent of lamb.
Three times I visited the shrine at Knock.
Our Lady was like an Aztec goddess.
I got lost once, wept for my mother.
Strangers pointed out the way to Mexico
where I might find my sacrificed father
but the sun's in the wrong direction. Nest,
I think not. Rather it is a stone's throw.

From my bedroom window I see Fahan Hill.
My grandfather said when the water touched
the base of that mountain the world would end.
Lisfannon is lonely, yet the human will
needs to stop the sea, for this place of rush
and rough grass gives in to the ocean's bend.
In the graveyard at Fahan Florence Nightingale's
friend lies waiting for her lover's Crimea,
a place of passion and war, the men pale
and frightened of women, Rachel and Leah.

The smell in the rose, the horn in the mouth,
the dead suffer from eternal drouth.

They pick and choose the sweet ones they desire.
They're Liquorice Allsorts, Smarties, barb wire.
They want to drink wild Sirocco orange.
They believe in the ordinary and strange.
They eat the Bible, devour the Koran.
They mix up the difference between woman
and man. They say, it's no matter to us,
we who have turned into extraordinary dust.

Best to leave the dead to their devices.
They're having a party in Valhalla.
Leave them to champagne, truffles and rice
that taste like spuds. They're jolly good fellows.
Imagine climbing Fahan Hill, Easter Sunday,
searching for eggs the Son of Man laid. Christ
is Russian, a Fabergé creation.
Orthodox priests, having gone astray,
end up in Donegal to worship the sun.
The stars misled them, they start to eat mice.

The priestly caste should always be feline.
Egyptian, they'd build pyramids of dulse.
My seven times round the world, my diamond mine,
Buncrana, my finger on my pulse,
you are life to me as life is a dream,
a madly eccentric millionaire's scheme
to light the whole town at the merest touch,
Harry Percival Swan, gift to the nation.
For this, rest and give thanks now the battle's won.
We'd seen the future was not up to much.

The border came and it went. So be it.
We looked outward, we looked inward. Big shite.
The only beautiful thing, purple Fahan Hill.
It watched us all and said nothing. The still,

silent music of Letterkenny. Dead,
my mother is dead. Hospital sorrow,
whose walls saw it before. Brother weeping,
sister quiet. Me, my brother, sister. Red,
all our hair. Her face the funeral tomorrow,
her body clematis window creeping.

That morning a miracle happened. Fahan Hill
erupted, volcanoes opened. My eyes
like lava solidified the Pound Lane
where she took breath to tell her story.
Always remember this is where you're from.
You kiss me cold, my daughter and my sons —
for Jesus' sake, am I now history?
Look, if you've a child, just give her my name.
That way I'll see to you. A drink, whisky,
Scotch, not Irish. I'll know when I'm full.

Juice from the bottle. Beware how you survive.
Look at you, looking at Fahan Hill. One night
the moon was mad, your mother was as well.
I was Jackie Kennedy Onassis.
The President himself, he was alive.
Though my heart broke I tried to do my best.
My cold Camelot, put to crazy flight,
your father a boat, my oceanic swell.
He was ghost to me but we took the risk.
For once in our lives no holding our *whisht*.
I know what you see stepping out our door.
We are Fahan Hill, Fahan Hill, where you were born.
We lead each other our lovely, long dance.
The living, the dead, what's the difference?

Sorn

Cart me to this playground,
arcade of wind and whin,
exchange my pence for silver
bird, and stream of tin.

The Stone Jug

Uncle Eugene caught salmon
beneath the Stone Jug
that looked at the Boys' Club
where they played indoor football.

Aunt Eileen sat in their car
but could drive like a native
through the townlands of home —
the Castle, the Cassie, Sorn.

One day a sheep crossed her road.
Get out of the way,
Jesus, I'm going to kill it.
She didn't.

But never again, Eugene,
behind the steering wheel of a car.
I can get there on my own two feet.
My stone jug, Aunt Eileen.

The Stone Jug: the last house between the River Crana
and Lough Swilly.

Cockhill

A famine in the churchyard
for godfearing bones;
at nights their tombstones bray,
and the master comes.

Fisherman

That catch could break the nets.
Pity the poor sea bream.
Pity the fisher of men.

Perhaps he made a bet.
Perhaps it was a dream.
Perhaps the pity is god and man.

Ardraven

Remembering a square cairn
in James Herron's field,
a buried horse or clustered well,
a river's silenced peal?

Perry Como

Will I ever forget the night his voice broke?
The carnival was over. But the people laughed
till they split their sides as he tried to sing.

Like a shirt torn or a broken pair of trousers
he was becoming a man, leaving me behind.
It happened outside the house but I heard it all

in the scullery rinsing clothes at the sink.
It was as if water was scurrying down the drain.
Him who this whole town nicknamed Perry Como.

How he stayed on the stage persisting, God knows.
But he started again and again. A nightmare.
I could do nothing for the son becoming a stranger.

One night in my sister's house, his voice came back.
Where had all the flowers gone, long time passing?
A cherry tree the Council had planted in my garden —

my world was going astray — I chopped the blossom,
the branch. The field opposite, my husband sang,
It's impossible. He'd be Perry Como.

Umracam

A bonefire of moss and meat,
five cows traverse this veldt.
What's restless in their motion?
Worn tracks where humans knelt.

Ivy

Chrissie O'Donnell — my cousin —
her house seared with ivy.
Why did that taste of kin —
the taste of green gravy?

PART TWO

Gyrfalcon

*'In West Clare an unusual avian visitor was spotted earlier
this month, a gyrfalcon.'*

— *The Irish Times*, January 2000

Hello

I think the parting was in the hello.
Too many years between, too many miles.
Too much weight, too little hair — the parting.

Drinking a glass of wine, the Trocadero,
your Mormon bones were red, your eyes the Nile.
(The goddess river of his laugh, I heard him sing.)

Sing, and the world starts with you. Then worlds change.
I did not know what globe you came from. Hard place,
where people say what they mean, sober, strange.
Their words sharpness, as strong as their face.

I think the parting was in the hello.
I think the hello was in the parting.

Someday when feeling low, I'll feel the glow.
I'm thinking of you. You. I am thinking.

Goodbye

Terminate my heart. Take power of feeling
from my left hand, my right hand. Drive a truck
through the window of the factory, my soul
works hard to make a living. You can chuck
aside to the wild four winds every thought
that this could end in anything but sin.
Investigate my love. Report it was shot.

Terminate my heart. A car chase through Brooklyn —
bullets through the dragon drug, my heart's desire.
When it's dead boil its head, my soup and bread.
But it's not dead, my boiled head, it's on fire.
Fire fucks you, fire insists, you must live instead.

Terminate my heart. Let me forget you,
as a red rose forgets the red, forgets the dew.

Leaves

Tomorrow night I'll dump out the black bags
from the bins in the back garden where leaves
are covering the place in their soft brown
habit of monks kicked from summer convents.

Poor shits, these sad leaves, once lovely, now hags
and withered. I tell them truly, you're mauve,
your looks have changed, don't let it get you down,
you've not been fooled, you know the way you went.

If you've had your day, that day was good, was great.
You fell of your accord. Summer took its toll.
To hell with winter, that's your reasoning.

I'd love to believe you. Then birds take wing,
fly up to heaven. And to hell with hell.
Hell is the heart breaking, grey leaf, like slate.

Rich

I've insulted the garden, pissed on the leaves.
There is more to this than a trash can.
There is more to my house than roars of grief.
I did it up, I became my own man.
If it is empty, it is because I —

I live by the sea, I never walk by the shore.
I stock the fridge with food I eat alone.
Rich men save, remembering they were poor.
In their trouser pocket gold turns to stone.
If they are empty pockets, it's because —

I've insulted the garden, pissed on the leaves.
There is more to my house than roars of grief.
I live by the sea, I never walk by the shore.
Rich men save, remembering when they were poor.

Poor

Nothing lives in the frozen wastes of ice.
Nothing a man of taste would like.

I came from the north and I knew the score.
I'm frightened of heights where the fall is sheer.

Say a bear were to touch you with its claws.
You need to be ready, act the hardchaw.

Have a tongue in your head that turns its stomach.
You be the strong man, the other be weak.

That's what's required from the poor in spirit.
Envy and lust and magnificent hate.

That's what's drummed into you when you are poor.
Smile in their face when you slam shut your door.

Be soft as butter but don't waste your breath.
Leave them to their life. Yourself to your death.

Butter and Tar

Don't soften me, man. That is what I ask.
I've learned the hard way how to wear a mask.
I've walked the floor at three in the morning,
toughening myself so I would not ring.
And the mask, it slipped, I lifted the phone.
Not you I called but the speaking clock.
I love that anonymous voice's pain.
Just like mine, seeing someone sucking cock.
It makes me think of tar and butter.
As boys playing football we used the latter.
Bare feet picked up melting dirt on the road.
That's where I played. In playing I showed.
That was home. A place that is near and far.
I was not happy, I was butter and tar.

The Jewish Bride

Say you were straight and found yourself a wife:
say the wedding ceremony were in the Frick.
I'd adorn you like the Jewish bride. Your man,
a bearded mystery, your dowry a knife.

I'd love that marriage of Mexican and Mick.
I have the fear of bread, wheat in your hand.

Say your honeymoon were spent counting gold,
gold that went into the making of your dress,
say that you were lonely reading the Cabala,
your Spanish soul looking over your shoulder,
what would it reveal — please, do let me guess —
you have never known what it's like to fall.

Adam and Eve, I think that's who you are.
You would not agree, and you would be right.
You're the Jewish bride. Mother, father,
husband, son and daughter, knife, day, night and light.

Survivor

My boat was crazy up the Amazon.
The engine went berserk and smelt of tuna.
Imagine my surprise. I was alone.

Alone in no man's land. My hands were fins.
I survived superbly. Alliteration
rowed me to a comfortable island.
I took my leisure there, fathered four sons.

Those boys were perfect. Bit the feeding hand.
When they slit me open, there was tuna.

They dined on my insides. Sweet cannibals.
This is all a dream. A fine waste of time.
Men learn the taste of fish. It is like walls
that surround the city no man enters.

Apart from the men who leave we call father.

Angelus

I swear this is true as there is no God.

Didn't the angel Gabriel appear to me?
An *amadán* of a fellow, wings like clods,
smelling of bog, and the butter would melt
on his forehead like ash, were he on fire,
were he milk churning in the dead sea.

That was not his intention. Not his desire.

He'd a message for me. Cover your pelt,
I ordered, to this naked messenger.
Why are you bollock naked, what brought you here?
A decent Donegal man needs no such song
as that which comes tripping from your tongue.

I said the wrong thing. Taking offence, he left.
Knew it was morning. You were light, my shaft.

Wings

Had I wings, I'd carry you to Kinnego Bay.
I wonder how it'd be to receive you there.

We'd drink sea water, we would eat seaweed.
I'd serve you good meat from Longwill's, the butcher.

But you are in America, far away.
America, that's broke many a mother's heart, I've heard.

Has it broke yours, my diamond, my need?

Neither, but the breaking of a rock against the sea.
Neither, but the sorrow that chooses not to speak.

Were it to beat, it could destroy the lovely sun.
Were it Kinnego Bay, it'd hold its tongue.

Had I wings, I'd carry you close against me.
Had I wings, you'd find out that they are weak.

Have I broke yours, my diamond, my sword?

Nine Times Nine

Nine times nine the days since I saw your eyes.
You're riding the subway going to work.
Nine times nine the heart beats in a day
missing a beat each time my bloody sark
is torn by a red rhino that wears its skin,
its savage horn to protect you from harm.

This creature lives in jungles. A sin
to tame it, cage it in light from the dark.
Like birds their wings are clipped, forget the sky.
What happens then? I think I know. Like men,
they marry. Married men are always shy.
They have their reasons, they devise a plan.

This involves changing flights, changing plumage,
hitting the streets, and begging for small change.

Mind

Mind yourself. In Donegal they say that.
Mind yourself. What will you mind, my lost one?
My lost one — you would dispute that hotly.
Dispute that hotly. You'd never say that.
Some days I heard your voice. They're not like nights.
The voices that tumble rapid from your mouth.
They come at me, all directions, east, south,
north, west. That's where they come from at night.
And I am lost, listening, listening.
I mind myself for the sake of you.
This winter's night, I wonder where are you?
Are you all right? Are you listening?
To what? To your own fear of you and me?
You'd never say that. Dispute that hotly.

Car

You can drive fast on the wrong side of the road.
I think that's your way, so I don't complain.
What would be the point? You'd never listen.

The way you are. That way makes you a man.
I wonder why it is I accept your pain.
I see you driving, but can't read the code.

Were you a lover, you'd be a driver.
Were you your sister, you'd be your logic.
You'll always drive on the wrong side of the road.
That's your way, so promise you'll not panic.

You're a frightening man, and you know it.
You're a frightening man, and you show it.
I see you in a car but can't read the code.
You can drive, I can't — wrong side of the road.

Law

Some nights I mistake you for someone else.
A man I love who left, eejit of a man.

Do you believe me when I'm lying — do you?
Lying is the smashing of Christmas delft.

My father falling down the stairs, Adam,
all too human. I remember all that's true.

It turns my stomach to tell you all this.
Some nights I mistake you for a man I kissed.

No, I don't. Not our way, it never was.
No lies. I've tried, Lord, to obey those laws.

Tonight I wish us together in Japan,
the temple gardens, you'd smell of jasmine.

I'd tell you tales of those who were loyal,
those who forgot, were mistaken and fell.

Malin Head

This is as far as this country takes you.
Ireland ends here, rocks like rams' pointed horns.
The ocean's a magnet, it pulls you northwards.

And the rocks, the ram, they look for the blue,
the red intoxicating stain of born
and being. This place, Malin Head, is hard.

I wish I could let you walk this landscape.
It has no fear of death. It invites flight,
gyrfalcon, my beautiful gyrfalcon,

you, my rock, my ram, my Malin Head, son
of the moon eclipsed by earth, my red night,
in my head tonight I think I will cope.

I'll go to my sleep and dream at my ease.
I wish all you wish, I wish you reason.

Horse's Head

Then the morning comes. My northern ice melts.
The terror comes back. Frightened of dying.
I recant all I confessed before. Sing
to me, let your lovely voice be the colt
to my mare, my mind, and nuzzle closely
to my breaking heart, to my breaking blood.

Why do I put you under lock and key?
Why don't I give you splendid drink and food,
not this mess of memory and remorse?

I am mountain and inedible gorse.
I set these plates on your delicate table.
They smell to high heaven, they stink of hell.

You are riding to work on the subway.
So I wake up, alive, and face the day.

Father Hegarty's Rock

Here's where the priest's head skipped across the grass
and never again did green show its face
on those spots where sacred blood was spilt. Places,
holy to the people I was born among,
you would find indifferent. If the last
shall be first, I'd crown you with the Song of Songs,
I'd martyr you with ungodly pleasures.
I would hear you crying, you would be hurt.

I won't show you Father Hegarty's Rock.
That's where they said Mass when it was outlawed.
Sacrament most holy, sacrament divine —

I believe only in what's rough, red and raw.
My god's a god you can rile, you can mock,
a god to disembowel, treacherous swine.

The Rhythm Boys

They are the big band my parents danced to.
They play that night in the Plaza Ballroom,
making a fist of 'The Way You Look Tonight'.

A fine tenor voice that might belong to you,
the town of Buncrana learning to swoon,
but something is strange, something's not right.

At three in the morning by the water's edge
a woman is walking, she is eight months gone.
Who does she see but a drowned boy running?
He has not gone home, nor taken his wages.

At four o'clock, sleeping in her bed,
her waters break, and the rest should be unsaid.
Suffice to admit he's her pride and joy,
drowning, dancing, one of the Rhythm Boys.

March

The year turning, the garden getting better.

This hotel room, London like a letter
sent home. I've smelt such rooms. Single beds, Florence.
Snoring in Paris. In Milan I danced
myself silly. Married man — wife, children
abandoned — he hurled bottles. Poisoned pen,
his crazy heart stopped strangers in the street
looking for his son, his white face a sheet
twisted between this mad father and myself,
fool, frightened stiff, being left on the shelf.
Wised up now, I leave such men to their fate.
Lovers once, they've aged, their hands empty plates.
This hotel room, London like a letter.

I phoned you. No answer. Getting better.

Oranges

Were I to bring you to a beautiful
hotel by Lake Como, laurel trees green,
oranges like the taste of fire, the hotel
would charge more than it's worth. I'd make a scene.

Pour wine over the waiter. Chew the fat
and spit it at the chef. Tell him to kiss
my Irish arse. Chicken tastes like a rat,
vegetables like snake — hear how they hiss.

How would you handle my misdemeanours?
You'd peel an orange and feed me the skin.
Like some lonely duke in a book of hours,
you'd be blue and golden eschewing sin.
I would be choking on the rind and pith,
celebrating the man I am not with.

With

He watches my every move, though he's not here.
Up to now I've cut him out. Then he appears.
He looks younger than his age. All agree.

He gives me licence, always has, I'm free
to fool myself. I'll come back, tail between
my legs, his dirty dog, his charlatan.
What did I imagine would have happened?
He would find out, get jealous, act real mean?

He says, I'm with you day, night — no secrets.
You'll get drunk and spill out your soul's sour milk.
Jesus, I'm tired out, I'm cold, I'm wet
with fucking lies. Truce, make up your mind. Risk
losing me. I watch every move you make.

He's not here. Never here. Never gives, takes.

Purgatory

Were you to die, go to Purgatory,
you would dazzle Jesus and His mother.
I can see the feast at Cana. Wedded
bliss between you and the son, altar wine
the like of which the Bible never told.
Stars guest from Hell. Slumming it from Heaven,
God would bless the union of His shy son.

Were you to die, go to Purgatory,
Jesus would convince His holy mother
your beauty deserved that it be wedded
to a perfect man, a man dined and wined
the like of which the Bible never told.
You'd be unhappy, knowing in Heaven
God would bless the union of His shy son.

Lie

When you lower your voice, it's baritone.
You could talk dirty and no one would hear.
That's when you move into magical zones.
Like a Japanese eel, you're what I fear.
It's quite sly, the way you know how to cruise.
You hide behind the mask of your laughter.
It is red. It is white. Like orange juice
I'd down you in one the morning after.
You know how long it is since I set eyes
on your face, scaring me? I burn photos
to forget. I set a match to my sighs.
I do not touch you. I never have. So,
these poems are lies. I need you like rain.
Meeting you, I could never be the same.

Truth

So, have you forgotten him? Yes, I have.
Of course he is doing well and I'm glad.
If I am in pain, it's my own doing.
A stupid fucker, I deserve to swing.
What came over me? I won't say I'm mad,
but was hungry for what I should not crave.
Let this be an end to crazy business.
Admit I was wrong and clean up the mess.
The other fella, he's getting on fine.
I'll not waste my own nor waste his hard time.
I wish him luck, I wish him all the best.
So have you forgotten him? Forgotten.
I'll get over this. I'll see a kestrel,
not my gyrfalcon, remembering when —

Sasparilla

I'll get you drunk on sasparilla,
get you roaring and happy, and come back,
you'll pierce your ear, you'll sing at every *fleadh*.
I'll explain the Irish meaning of crack.
We'll trek through Kerry and dark Donegal.
I'll feed you oysters, mussels and roe.
You'll sate yourself on kidneys, sweet offal
smelling of honeycomb where praties grow.
I'll blight you with this country's civil war.
Had you brother you'd turn against brother
and sister. Forget father and mother.
Worship the god who loves murder and drunkard.
That's what I offer to strangers I love.
This country for you. We give what we have.

Shamrock

This Patrick's Day wear these lines as a badge.
The shamrock is threefold: love, hate and lies.
Dig a deep grave, light a big fire. Burn bones,
remove all trace of the past. Some chance, sweetheart.
I'll tell you how they make Fermanagh fadge.
They spit in the dough, the raisins are sties
trapped in the pupils of blue rocks and stones.
They see forever. Their breath is a wart
scalding the lids of leprous eyes, blind
to their failings, failings much like a man
who gives his blessing this holy saint's day.
All he asks from you is you keep in mind
this warning: I live in no holy land.
The shamrock is threefold: rock, famine and clay.

Clay

I can't bring you to Donegal. I've stood
by my parents' grave. I can't let you see
this sorrow. Forgive me, I'm a coward.
I've not mourned enough. Were I shedding blood,
it would not pay back — the leaves from the trees
in the garden last winter. It is still hard,
it will always be hard. Mother, father,
the grave opens, it will never close.
I'm telling these secrets to a stranger.
They'd love him, the cut of him, his smiles, his clothes.
August, October, I'm frightened of the fall.
Forgive me, I cannot bring you to Donegal.

Roar

Roar me out of this. It will not work, mate.
The ice is melting. You can't stop the thaw.
I'm a neutral country. Always have been.
I pride myself that neither love nor hate
can stop this grief. It is a form of hate
to remember what might have been.
I would like a flood to banish the thaw
that threatens me now. I am not your mate.
Still, I continue to write to you. Lost,
alone, fearing being alone and lost,
what started out as a way of saving
myself, damning myself, treacherous, know
this above all else, I always say no,
I'm in the business of losing, saving.

Dream

Five in the morning, not able to sleep,
were I to dream, it would not be of you,
no more than we walked beside the ocean.
I'm glad we never walked together there.
That way neither the water nor Irish Sea
would sound like you, the way you look tonight.
I should go to bed. I dread not dreaming.
The gyrfalcon in my head's spreading his wings.
Where the hell in the world's he taking flight,
I'll leave it up to him. What will be will be.
I can say for sure your soul is not here.
So let the music be raucous, pure *sean nós*.
Were it to dream, it would not be sky blue.
Five in the morning, not able to sleep.

Dreaming

No dream — this happened. I was innocent —
can you believe that? A ten bob note, babe,
monkey nuts, apples and oranges, coconut,
jars of honey, cotton candy, labels
of October, the last night of October,
when witches and warlock disturb my sleep
even though I was abed in Dublin —
one Hallowe'en my da won a hamper.
We spent a fortune in celebration.
Sober Mormon, you do sow as you reap.
What's the meaning of innocence, of sin?
Are we always, always our father's sons?
I'd like to think not. Enlighten me, man.
Do you believe in God? Some other man.

The Bali Sea

We can drink safely in the Bali Sea.
The border's a mile beyond, get away
quickly. Should they raid, we'll down our brandies
and ginger, hitch up our pants and we'll fly
to where the law is strictly our making.
In New York they gathered at the Stonewall,
so many are ghosts, there for the taking,
a voodoo disease caught them by the balls.
We're drinking safely in the Bali Sea.
Derry erupting, it's four miles away.
Men and their wives drink with the men's lovers.
The lovers are standing the wives large brandies.
Drink like a fish, drowning your sorrows dry,
keep your wits, watch the door, she's my cover.

St Roche

Were we ever to be one, table talk,
finishing our sentences, silence would reign.
The same table would serve different dishes.
Our horses stabled with the one rope, they'd shock
the company with their serene fucking.
It would be decorous, a sublime pain.
Not our way, not our wisdom, not our wish.
We would feed the horses with clean water, sweet
as nights that never happened. Never will.
Human flesh, the oats we'd give their fill.
Generous to a fault, we would then wing
our way out of this, we're smart, we can cheat.
I'd look at and love you. I'd crack a joke.
I'd be happy, showing my wounds — St Roche.

Laughter

We've had a child that I gave to strangers.
It was better than aborting, I'm told.
You would not agree and she has your laugh.
We've had a child and I gave it away.
I was young, you were escaping the draft.
I went to Amsterdam. Europe was cold.
The frozen canals, they were like your laugh.
We had a child and I gave it away.
I went speed-skating and ended up drowned.
They buried me in the old cathedral.
Catholics slept there with Protestants. Where
will she search for me, blind child reading Braille?
We had a child, creature of sight, of sound.
We had a child and I gave it away.

Glove

I will meet him in the festival club,
his dutiful wife silent beside him,
waiting for her drunk husband to rear up.
Dutifully, he does so. Time to snub
the arrogant bastard who dared to sup
of better wine. Sad how he's turned out prim.
Prim and proper, she does keep the boy well.
I lay with you, you left, that's what he shouts.
It's true, I did so because you bored me.
You left me because you knew I would tell
there was nothing in my heart, wanted out
before you took the earth from me, the sea.
You were never earth nor sea. What you loved
you never wanted, your heart, finger, glove.

Nightmares

At least I paid for myself in Florence.
Those purple hills outside Pisa, you wept
that first time to see them. I loved your dense
Donegal soul. What nightmares have we slept
together? You left me for an English guy.
I always knew he would be someone older.
This American, he is your fantasy.
He doesn't want you. A cruel shoulder,
that's now where you'll shed your tears. Fermanagh
reared me to tell the truth. My hair cut short,
I now finger the black secret of bra.
I know the way to destroy you, to hurt.
I am the one most beautiful to look at.
Beautiful, beautiful, remember that.

Ibsen in Winter

Henrik Ibsen fell in love with a young girl.
An old fella, he womaned himself, pearled
his neck and asked the gentle guillotine
to take his soul and save the lonely queen
he saved from ever knowing his desire.
The young one told Ibsen to pull his wire,
get a grip, who the hell was he fucking
in his dreams? She was not into sucking
his stick of Bergen rock, wise up, old man.
He heard her answer. It was apple flan
to a hungry mind, starved of sugared cloves.
He loved the way she mocked his horn and hoofs.
He was the devil, she was salvation,
she was Satan, he was angel and drum.

Drum

I make a loud noise, constant percussion.
Loud as it is, I feel I hide behind
the music of what's missing. Fingers and thumbs,
I know ten times ten is a hundred. Mind
has ways of catching up with itself. Break
your heart lamenting what you fear might be,
show your wounds to the world. I'd say broken
heart is better than broken mind. You're free
to run the riot act through the chaos
of my past. Shite's symphony, dirt's orchard,
I fade, I sour, I'm past who gives a toss.
The music of what's missing, savage and hard.
In my mind you start singing. My body
hears. It does not dance. It sways. Body's free.

Prog

Buncrana word — prog.
Prog, stealing apples,
boys careering over Louis O'Kane's
wall and being caught, he would make you say
an Act of Contrition. A good fellow,
he believed in God, Mass every day,
I remember Louis, I love his name.

Why am I making acts of contrition
to a man I barely know, I barely met?
Because I'm stealing apples in time's fog
I hoped covered me. Idiot, I bet
you'll listen, gamble — then daylight comes.

You don't gamble, don't smoke. You have no shame.
I like you for that. I like your lack of pain.

Pain

None of us learned to drive, my father's sons.
Americans are shocked at us. They hire
cars and drive to Galway. Part of the fun
of being in Ireland is how close desire
is to destruction. We look like tramps,
the Irish, next to you. Torn pullovers,
trousers with flies open, feasting on champ
and bad liver, we look like a shower
of knackers out for the day, a wedding
that should never have happened, but it did.
That's why the Irish have millions of kids —
fertile as bogweed, ripe for the bedding,
accidents waiting to happen, hit, run.
None of us learned to drive, my father's sons.

You

The goodbye was sore, but it was honest.
I vowed to leave you and meant what I said.
Never meeting again would be all right.
So fuck off yourself, this is for the best.

If I believed that, I'd believe the nights
were for the birds, believe debts were paid
years before they send in the bailiffs. You
come back to me some mornings. I'm awake.
My honeyed tongue singing, singing the blues.
Wasp stinging my arse, you'd not let me fake
what I feel about you. I don't know
who you are. I don't want to, but I do.
This is my way of saying how are you?
My eternal goodbye, fervent hello.

Ghost

Five hours from now you'll be asleep, safe, sound.
The yellow cabs will still be working hard.
You could be driving a man who is drowned,
big as Neptune, a god with a calling card.
Bring him where he wants to go. In sleep, take
him and his lady wife, somewhere, nowhere —
they have an address in the Village. Dare
you to drop them where they stand. Say a lake
in Central Park where the god ghost met the ghost
of his lover, pushed under a train, north-
bound, years ago, and his shadow was roast
meat, a Sunday dinner, the gravy froth
from his mouth. I know that man. He is bound
to pull you under. I don't want you drowned.

Damned

The sorrow in the sun gave birth to fire.
It knew it would always be rekindled.
Did you come from heaven or from hell?
Did you spring from air, did you spring from mire?
Where are you from? Is it good? Is it bad?
I'd say you leapt from angels, tormenting
daemons, hurling them out from crazy shadows,
pitch black, desperate to hide their lost wings.

They flap, these wings, they beat, fucking eejits,
afraid of falling in love with angels.
They get sense then — remember this conceit.
No human soul has known heaven, hell.
Death is incomprehensible. You come
from where, I ask myself. Where'd you come from?

Father

The day of your death I'll lie beside my lover
and weep on his shoulder for the death of my father
I've never known. That will be my father's death.

The day of his death I lay beside my lover
and wept on his shoulder for my death of the father
he'd never known. That would be our fathers' death.

Since the day our father died I've lost track of time.
I no longer believe in reason nor rhyme.
I let him down in every single respect.
He'd be glad that's so, locked round my neck.
So why does he come knocking at my floor
where there's no one to open the open door?
Why do I go to his grave and speak to him,
we who never spoke, why do we begin?

Lover

My lover I mentioned, I mentioned him.
The father that fashioned me. Out on a limb.
They remind me why I'm on this good earth.
I know them both. I know you. What you're worth.
I could buy none of you — fuck what money
brings. Lover, father, yourself — I do try
to stay faithful. I belong to a church
whose sin is loss of face, a crazy lurch
and desperate grope. I will not do that.
I'm frightened of my falcon's strong wings. Let
them beat their music, not mine. Lover, hurt
by these poems, I rub your face in dirt.
I wish they would stop. There's no stopping them.
Love is the paradox of now, soon and when.

Fate

Say no more of whatever's understood.
Things spoken out of order, nothing good
could come of this but the loss of faith.
Value the man who's stood by you. You are both.
The falcon does not need your nest. Don't blame
the poor shitehawk that you've christened his name.
Jesus, where in Christ did gyrfalcon spring?
It's like something foreign he's suffering.

No, he thrives where he finds a mate.
I caught sight of him after he'd flown.
It does not matter if history or fate
dictates to him if he's loved or alone.
He can survive extremes of love or cold.
That's what he tells me. I believe what I'm told.

Possessed

The gyrfalcon cannot be possessed.
That's the basic wisdom of his feathers.
If he could laugh, then he would laugh but shan't.
I adore the way the gyrfalcon is dressed.
Coat of single colour, right for all weathers,
he'll suit the Mardi Gras, perfect for Lent.
His sins are few, his perfection plenty,
I'd say he owns this room. That's his country.

I've no more control over that fine beast
than I have control over his flight east
to where he mates with phoenix, turtle, snake,
and all the errors my gyrfalcon makes,
with his present, his past, his winged future.
He's a diamond, he's rich, he has the cure.

Run

Were I sitting at a bar drinking wine
after wine, you came in, order water —
we would not show any interest.
Remain in silence the whole long night.
You looking at your handsome reflection,
I'd like your vanity, your loneliness.

Were you sitting at the bar wasting time
and I came in swearing blindly you swore
your love for me, it would be for the best
you looked askance, raised your eyes to heaven,
smiled, cursed the Irish, remembered a fight
you came out on top and thanked God you're blessed
to be better than the average man.
Not you. Never. You'd be smart. You'd run.

Orchids

Say for your prom I gave you orchids,
flowers that would last till you let them die,
strange purple orchids, flowers without smell,
like yourself without definition —

but the giving was good, no one could tell
that these were love between man and man —

                                                        try

as I might I cannot imagine you won
over by flowers — a tough and wise kid.

What were you like when you were younger?
I'd guess unapproachable — raw and red
inside the brown flesh you hide to the world.
You saw the world stare and you returned the stare.
You were white — expensive — and in your head
you deserve the best — no man better dare.

Herbs

Being away from you, it's hard to describe.
Were you in Ireland, you'd enjoy tonight.
The mad flowers thrive beneath the window.
There's a burst of whatever's bursting right
where it should be flourishing. It's a robe
like a cartoon remembered. The year flows
into another notion. I'd noticed
nothing for a long time till you arrived.
You can blame me for saying the long list
of herbs. Rosemary, tarragon, sage, chives.
They smell of you. They want you to come back,
it's up to yourself. At least, this I planned.
Should you want this garden in your palm's hand,
I promised it won't turn to weeds and brock.

Leg

Some are given three wishes, I got three blows.
That's this business for you. Follow your nose,
it will smell the flowers and devilish thorns.
Since you're not here, the white page will suffice
to let you know I'm managing. In Sorn
they're cutting the turf, in China eating rice.
Me, I'm somewhere between the east and west.
A globe in my house shows me where you are.
I'm tempted to call you but why the heck
should a man disturb your beautiful rest?
Your parents had plans for their son. You're reared
to be good. You're always here. For your sake
I ask silence, that wonderful friend, to beg
you destroy desire, a leg touching leg.

East

Were you here, I'd be lost and so would you.
I don't believe in the fortunes men tell
each other in the dark of night. It's well
a man faces up to his destiny,
but the gods declare better not be born
than wish yourself to another's pleasure.
I don't believe that. I believe in blue
China that reads the willow-patterned future.
I went into town and I had my hair shorn.
A Japanese widow, I would be free
of my husband's ghost, but it is haunting
the bed I try to sleep on, it comes back
and I'm dutiful, clipping my own wings,
and don't fly to what it is my heart lacks.

West

The ghost took body last weekend. We fucked,
the living and the dead. The living was the dead.
The morning after I dined on bacon,
toasted bread. I knew I'd committed sin.
I'd enjoyed it. You could call it the luck
of the Irish. No two were ever wed
but one has a sorrow, people reckon.
That wisdom has the ring of loss and gain.
It's all down to fear of dying, I guess;
the way we lead our lives not together.
A preparation for being alone.
It's a comfort to think that what we bless
will be constant as stone, as the weather
that shapes the rain and the loneliest star.

Paint

So long since I saw you, I remember
distinctly all about you. Your black hair
that touched cold as sleet before falling soft
on streets in New York last November.
Your fine legs climbing the stairs to a loft
where rich bastards banished with practised flair
all trace of furniture like Wittgenstein
from his house in Vienna. There white walls
like the shirt that smells of you put a shine
on the empty tract of his life. Fools
walk in and decide a lick of paint
is just what this joint needs. You're not a saint
but you're a holy man when the time's right.
Right to leave, avoid scenes, and have no fights.

Fists

I'd love to see you lose your temper
and go hell for leather against a man,
who crossed you in a poker game you played,
for no more reason than you felt like it.
How would your hands contract into fists, square
and domiciled in the suburbs of towns
where no woman's safe, where buffalo stray
through streets that smell of a frightened boy's wit?
Wit saved him often from the bullies' blows,
it made him laugh — he could see through their clothes.
Naked and gentle, they were not transformed.
As nature intended, yellow as corn,
they did not embrace, they stood far apart,
sensing blood in the game of spades and hearts.

Judge

Are you ever in? Are you always out?
I'm packing for London. Tomorrow night
I'll don jacket, tie, eat at the Connaught.
They serve roast beef, on the bone, red. I'm white,
I'm hungry, also red, red all over
apart from my love, who is not covered
red, if I say so myself, though I'm no judge.

I caught sight of your soul one day. Shyly,
I turned cartwheels and was consumed by bad thoughts,
the way you are consumed by chocolate.
Why do we love the sweet impulse we hate?
Could I answer that, then I would be free,
but I'm not, no more than you. You I sought.
If I say so myself, I'm my own judge.

Apples

Working rough into the night I take a break.
I think about calling you but I don't.
You're not there, never there, like himself.
That's what binds you. Self-centred men I love.
You worship the mirror, that poisoned apple.
What do you see in it but ageing men?
The two of you touch, you are both on the make.
You like what you are, you love as you want.
You would leave me in the circles of hell,
but I'd find my fucking way out. I love
two dark angels who are savages, cruel.
Flaying's too good for these two bastards who plan
to kill whoever's told their true stories.
Kill him who ruins our histories.

Aisling

In the morning light I find I calm down.
In an aisling, my lover, beautiful
and shapely, becomes the map of England.

He is foreign and prone to sleeping sound
while I throw a fit and roar, I've my fill
of doing my duty, I've done handstands
in the service of this love that's lasted.

Can we not wipe the slate clean and start again?
He looks through rose-coloured spectacles. Shame
on you for mocking a man that tasted
the trials, tribulations of your life.

You forget I stood beside you like Ireland,
and England, happy marriage. Husband, wife.
Together for eternity. Sea, sand.

End

There is wine in the fridge and the cellar,
but this party has to end. You don't drink
but you're broken to the bone to be involved
in this particular mess. Irish fags
are a breed apart. Their English partners
deserve what's coming. You did not ask for
this invitation. You'd like some fresh air.

Jesus, aren't you the regular fellow?
So lucky you'd float were your ship to sink.
Think back on me and I'm the problem solved.
You would not be so hard. I try to drag
you down to the level where I compare
you to daemons I've lost and loved. No more.
I've to let you go. I wish you were here.

Clean

What is here? A clean house, I try my best.
In New York they drink coffee and sugar,
I poured salt into my cup. See how much
I miss you. Smart guy, you would know the touch
I'm aiming for. I wish you peace and rest
after tough work. I know you work so hard.
Many reasons to love you, I'll mention one.
The way you fight to make a clean living.
You come from a breed of honest people.
In that respect I think I do know you well.
They love you as I do, with some passion.
You're smart, you're honest, you're the one giving.
You take my breath away. You always have.
You're something else. Aren't you? I should leave.

Soon

So soon until I see you, your birthday
to celebrate. That salad of pink cake
and the sugar on fire.
                        I could hold sway
at the do, an excellent MC. Break
a leg, I mean it and I really do.

A joke, a dirty joke, a man giving
rein to his fantasies, what I have done
with my life will not lead to heaven.
I am frightened of finishing this book.
When it ends I might end, though I doubt it.

Had it an index of wisdom and wit,
I would devour it, wings, feather and beak.
My gyrfalcon, I'm starting out again,
enraged, emotional, impulsive, stained.

PART THREE

The Wife's Lament

The Wife's Lament

My husband made millions and disappeared,
but it was me who suffered banishment
for I was absent from his tortuous bed
where I conceived the rich snake, the necklace
he wove around my face, pure mother-of-pearl.
I listened to his operatic dirge,
the endless saga of how he understands
my needs, my necessities — a woman wants
what she can have if the scan shows a son
is dancing wildly, her belly full of cock.
His jewel shines in my night's pure darkness
and it lights my way back to where I'm from,
where my father, the King, constructed bridges
to realms where mother exercised control —
she mastered him, he asked her, she gave.
Nothing but death came between my parents.
They caught him marauding in their bedroom
and ripped the flesh off death, his hairy scales
that smelt of vinegared fish, my husband's
smell. He came for me across the ocean.
A well brought up girl, I waited. Orders
came that none be spared. Like all the rest, I'd be
killed unless I married. I married.
The flower of sweet Strabane, lily of the valley,
Rose of Sharon, I perfumed that strange male.
He bought me a mobile home outside Moate
in the county of Westmeath, while I longed
for gypsy caves near Galway where women
tamed their feral claws by scratching the poles
of virgins that left their family too early.
My husband, my overlord, made millions.
We had children. He bought them bungalows
and furnished with ivory crosses the rooms
girls gave birth in, his daughters who loved him.
One died in Spain, shortage of breath, childbirth.

As though our love, our marriage had never been,
we lived together a long time in the peace
that passed understanding, the quiet bed
his size took too much shape in where we slept
like strangers, like Cromwell's soldiers sleeping.
Awake, they'd knock me round the shop. I bought
my freedom once, a gown of golden fishskin
torn from my husband's back, paid for with his wages
sweated from the brow of his river red
forehead, his brain a dying daughter — stop,
I've said before I cannot talk about that.
About his career, I was part and parcel,
the little hen that would lay the golden egg.
I smashed my face against mirrors. Silver
were my veins. My husband was out screwing
younger girls who hung around the mobile home
in Moate. When he died they all vanished.
I suppose they were sorry. May grief always attend
girls who long still for their lousy, lost beloved.

The Husband's Message

1

On Booterstown Strand the revolution
involved the discovery of the moon's
changing shape into the diurnal sun
that took its vocation when fate was soon.
It was owed serious holiday pay —
wars put beyond bounds any strike action.
Still, always one insisted on his say.
This soldier wrote letters from the front.
Bastard. In his country people live alone.
Letters came through windows like covenant stone.
We believe in commandments God has described
as fitting manners for our holy tribes
who decipher the meanings carved on trees,
the silver birch, oak, yew and mulberry.

2

In this country people live apart. Their choice.
They set fire to themselves and their neighbours.
They'll drive to death in a golden Rolls Royce
and recite their songs from long lost folklore.

When I believed my sins were forgiven
I was inclined to forget where I was born
among the trees that sheltered the mad wren
sent from strange lands where plenty dropped its horn

into milk and honey. Now I have come
over idiotic seas and I must find out
how in your hearts you feel towards the sons
of my lords who went missing in riots

over what went wrong between our peoples.
Are they alive or have you cut their throats?
That is your way, but know there'll be hell
in our hearts, the bottomless pockets of coats

where we keep our purse, our suicide bombs.
We've smelt their bodies in your hidden runes.
We know where you hide your cattle and lambs.
We will be avenged for strong and puny.

We will be avenged for Adam and Eve.
The trees in your garden will turn winter
to winter. No tales from miller or reeve
will soften with laughter what lies in store.

Your lord is waiting for your homecoming.
He is waiting across terrible water.
You board a ship and I wish it strong wings.
You will know peace, you will die in water.

Almighty God, grant you all you desire.
My lord listens to your heartfelt requests.
Should your daughters add fuel to his fire,
He will destroy you, north, south, east and west.

3

Thus wrote the soldier in his epistle.
Friends, enemies could only wish him well.
They believed their sins were forgiven
singing in trees sheltering the mad wren.

Cure

I give him what he needs. Aquamarine
to make black out of blue that contradicts
both. There's wine to drink and gin.
He owes a fortune. The candle's wick
illuminates a woman losing milk.
That wagon knows how to use her fists.
Brothers-in-law tear their mother's silk.
The way he works with fingers and wrist,
he knows the magic of the hand
touching what it needs to touch. Sad wanker,
he is Martha and Mary. Rands
from South Africa would be his banker
had he lived to tell the tale.
My booklets of gold leaf, linseed oil,
turpentine from Venice, I make the sale.
He buys. I know he's God's spoilt
child, but I say nothing.
The day he touched my eyes, I was damned.
He was the blue that black brings.
Lapis lazuli from Afghanistan.

Riddle

They settled here, but did not breed.
They brought jewellery and chains.
The women went untouched.

The men they loved, marriage
between man and master. Brain
touched brain, an idea seeded.

Seize the day and rage.
Be my love, be too much.

They listened to this heresy.
We decided to have babies.
Kept our mouths shut at birth.
They discovered we were enemies.
We cured their cocks with rabies.
We cursed, gave them the earth.

Elegy

I suppose that Hatch Street is empty.
Nobody lives in houses there anymore.
Certainly not after this brutal news.
Who could go into St Stephen's Green?

I hear the flowers have abandoned the beds.
The ducks, purple and blue, drowned in water.
They've woken from a very bad dream.
Eileen O'Sullivan has strayed from the path.

I see her walking through an open front door;
she's singing they can't take that away from me.
Maybe because her reason like her hair is red
she fought the frequent battles that she fought.

Her dreams were what made that strange woman.
Her love was the devil she understands.

Gardens in Winter: A Charm

December fourth, your birthday.
The purple cosmos thrives.
Our bodies sway.
Our bed a plate of knives and knives.